D1262880

AMAZ AMAZING SCIENCE ENCE

AMAZING SCIENCE
AMAZING
ELECTRICITY

Sally Hewitt

 Crabtree Publishing Company
www.crabtreebooks.com

Crabtree Publishing Company
www.crabtreebooks.com

Editors: L. Michelle Nielsen, Michael Hodge
Senior Editor: Joyce Bentley
Senior Design Manager: Rosamund Saunders
Designer: Tall Tree

Photo Credits: Helene Rogers/ Art Directors: p. 21; Jim Craigmyle/Corbis: p. 7; Rick Gomez/Corbis: p. 13; Louis K. Melsel Gallery Inc./Corbis: p. 18; Roy McMahon/Corbis: p. 3, p. 9; Roger Ressmeyer/Corbis: p. 17; Royalty-Free/Corbis: p. 27; Alison Wright/Corbis: p. 16; Getty Images: cover, p. 8; George Grall/Getty Images: p. 14; Peter Hendrie/Getty Images: p. 26; Thomas Hoeffgen/Getty Images: p. 19; Fernand Ivaldi/ Getty Images: p. 12; Lester Lefkowitz/Getty Images: p. 11; Pascal Le Segretain/Getty Images: p. 20; Jeremy Liebman/Getty Images: p. 25; Chris Mellor/Getty Images: p. 10; Henning von Hollenben/Getty Images: p. 24; Mike Golka: p. 15; NASA: p. 6; Philip Wilkins: p. 22, p. 23

Activity & illustrations: Shakespeare Squared pp. 28-29.

Cover: A lightning bolt hits Sugar Loaf Mountain in Rio de Janeiro.

Title page: Static electricity causes a girl's hair to stand on end.

Library and Archives Canada Cataloguing in Publication

Hewitt, Sally, 1949-
    Amazing electricity / Sally Hewitt.

(Amazing science)
Includes index.
ISBN 978-0-7787-3610-3 (bound)
ISBN 978-0-7787-3624-0 (pbk.)

    1. Electricity--Juvenile literature. I. Title. II. Series:
Hewitt, Sally, 1949- . Amazing science.

QC527.2.H49 2007   j537   C2007-904307-0

Library of Congress Cataloging-in-Publication Data

Hewitt, Sally, 1949-
    Amazing electricity / Sally Hewitt.
        p. cm. -- (Amazing science)
    Includes index.
    ISBN-13: 978-0-7787-3610-3 (rlb)
    ISBN-10: 0-7787-3610-5 (rlb)
    ISBN-13: 978-0-7787-3624-0 (pbk)
    ISBN-10: 0-7787-3624-5 (pbk)
    1. Electricity--Juvenile literature. I. Title.
    QC527.2.H58 2008
    537--dc22
                                        2007027423

Crabtree Publishing Company
www.crabtreebooks.com   1-800-387-7650

Printed in the USA/122009/CG20091229

Published in Canada
Crabtree Publishing
616 Welland Ave.
St. Catharines, ON
L2M 5V6

Published in the United States
Crabtree Publishing
PMB 59051
350 Fifth Avenue, 59th Floor
New York, New York 10118

Contents

Amazing electricity

Electricity gives power to lights and machines. Lights are so bright in big cities that they can be seen from space.

Electricity is a kind of **energy**. It gives lights energy to shine.

Electricity gives machines the energy to work. Electric heaters which the energy to heat.

YOUR TURN!

What machines at your home use electricity to work?

Computers need electricity to work.

Natural electricity

Lightning is natural electricity. It is seen as huge sparks or bolts flashing between storm clouds and the ground.

Lightning is a kind of electricity called "**static** electricity".

When a balloon is rubbed against a person's hair, static electricity is made.

Static electricity causes a girl's hair to be pulled toward a balloon.

YOUR TURN!

Rub a balloon on a cloth made of wool. The static electricity will make the balloon stick to the wall.

Making electricity

Electricity is made at **power plants**. Oil, gas, or coal is often burned at these plants to turn water into steam.

Turning water into steam creates energy. This energy is turned into electricity.

Energy from the sun, wind, and moving water is also used to make electricity.

YOUR TURN!
Do you think that it is better to make electricity by burning oil, gas, and coal or by using the power of the sun, wind, and water?

The spinning blades on these wind **turbines** help make electricity.

Using electricity

Electricity makes machines work. It makes lights flash, escalators move, and radios play.

Electricity **flows** from power plants along **cables**. The cables come into buildings. Sockets in walls let people plug in machines.

To make a machine work, you have to plug it in and turn it on.

YOUR TURN!

What would stop working at your home if the electricity was turned off?

Electricity flows along a **wire** into a hairdryer to make it work.

SCIENCE WORDS: **cable   flow**

13

Danger!

An electric eel uses electricity as a weapon to protect itself or hunt for food. It can kill other animals for food with an electric **shock**.

Electricity can be **dangerous**.
A strong electric shock could
hurt or even kill a person.

Electricity flows through water,
making the water dangerous
to touch.

Electricity does not flow through
plastic. Bathroom light **switches**
are made of plastic. They protect
you from getting a shock.

SCIENCE WORDS: **dangerous   shock**

Moving along

An electric train speeds along a track. An electric **rail** on the ground gives it the power to move.

Electric trains have big **motors** that use a lot of electricity.

Toy trains have small motors that use only a small amount electricity.

Electricity runs through the railway tracks into the toy train.

YOUR TURN!

Find things at home that need electricity to move. Do they move in a straight line or around in circles?

Batteries

These toy **robots** light up, talk, and move. They get their energy from **batteries**.

Batteries are power packs for small machines that do not use much electricity.

Batteries make electricity when the machines are turned on.

A battery gives this flashlight the power to shine.

YOUR TURN!

Find things that use batteries to work.

SCIENCE WORDS: **battery robot**

On and off

Turning on one **switch** can light up thousands of colored lights. All of the lights are **joined** by electric wires.

When you turn on a light switch, electricity flows along wires and lights up the light bulbs.

When you turn the switch off, electricity stops flowing, and the lights go out.

Switches on walls often power lights but can also power other things, such as ceiling fans.

YOUR TURN!

Find electric switches on the walls and on machines. Just look, don't touch!

SCIENCE WORDS: switch   wire   join

Make a circuit

Electricity flows through wires in a circle, or **circuit**. Ask an adult to help you make a simple circuit.

You need a light bulb, a light bulb socket, or holder, two wires with clips, and a battery pack.

Join one end of each wire to the battery pack. Join the other ends to the light bulb socket.

YOUR TURN!

Can you explain why the light goes out when the circuit is broken?

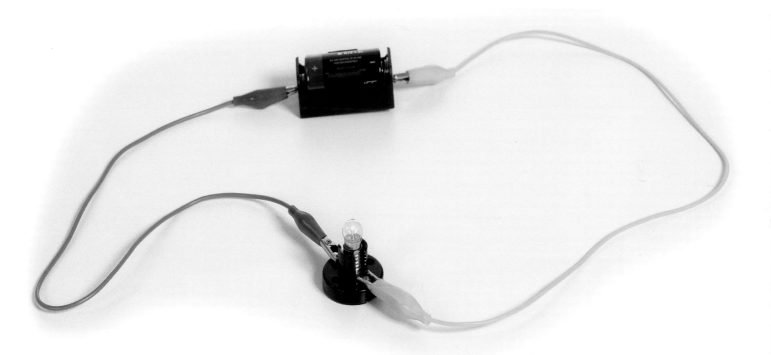

The circuit is complete when the wires are joined to the battery and socket, causing the light bulb to shine. The bulb goes out if you **break** the circuit.

SCIENCE WORDS: **break   circuit**

Life without electricity

When people camp, they often do not use any electricity. They light **fires** for cooking and keeping warm.

Electricity was first used in homes about 100 years ago.

Before electricity, people lit fires for cooking and washed clothes and cleaned dishes by hand.

YOUR TURN!

Do you that think washing, rinsing, and wringing out your clothes is hard work? Try it and see!

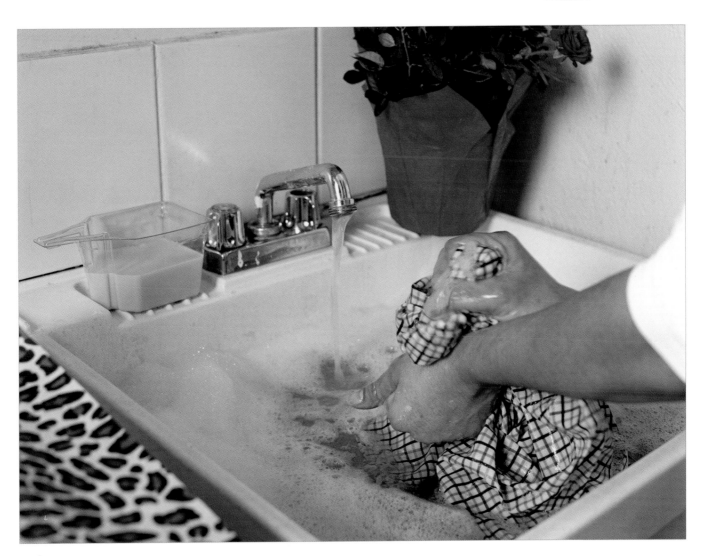

Washing clothes by hand can be **hard work**.

SCIENCE WORDS: **fire   hard work**

Save electricity

Burning oil, gas, and coal to make electricity fills the air with dirty smoke. One day these **fuels** will run out.

We **waste** a lot of electricity at home and school every day.

Saving electricity helps keep the air cleaner.

Doors and windows should be closed to keep heat in homes and buildings.

SCIENCE WORDS: fuels save waste

The tang of electricity

Try this experiment to feel the effects of electricity.

What you need

- one lemon
- a penny
- a dime
- paper
- a glass of water
- a pencil
- a ruler
- an adult to help

1. Roll the lemon around on the top of a desk, pressing down on it with your hand as you do. Roll the lemon around several times, and shake it, too.

2. Ask an adult to help you by cutting two short slits next to each other on the top of the lemon. Each slit should cut through the skin of the lemon and be about 3/4 inches (2 cm) long. The slits need to be about 1/2 inch (1.27 cm) apart.

3. Push the dime halfway down into one slit on the lemon. Push the penny halfway down into the other slit.

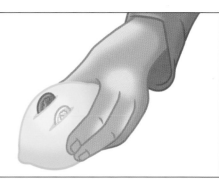

4. Dip your index finger in the glass of water to wet it. With your wet finger, touch both the penny and the dime at the same time. What happens? Did you feel a jolt? Try this experiment a few times. Write down what you felt.

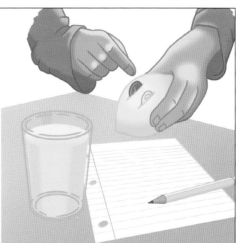

What happened:

When you rolled the lemon around, you "turned on" the battery inside. That battery is really the acid in the fruit, or the juice that makes a lemon taste tangy. When you put in the dime and the penny, you were giving your lemon battery a way to let that electricity out, like the plus and minus signs that all batteries have on their ends. Water is a great carrier of electricity—which is why rain and lightning often occur together. When you connected the plus-side and minus-side coins with your wet finger, you felt the jolt of the natural electricity that rolling the lemon produced!

Glossary

batteries   Power packs that make electricity. Batteries give things such as flashlights, radios, and clocks the power to work.

break   When something breaks, it comes apart in pieces. When an electric circuit breaks, the wires come apart, and electricity cannot flow through them.

cables   Thick wires. Electricity flows along cables from power plants into our homes.

circuit   A circuit is a loop or a circle. Electricity flows around in a circuit.

dangerous   Something that is dangerous can hurt you. Electricity can be dangerous if you do not use it safely.

electricity   A kind of energy that we use to give things the power to work.

energy   Energy, such as electricity, gives things the power to work.

fires   Fires burn and give out heat and light.

flow   A way of moving along. Water flows out of a tap. Electricity flows along wires.

fuels   Materials from the ground, such as oil, gas, or coal, that are made into energy.

hard work   Work is a job that has to be done. You use a lot of energy to do hard work.

joined When things are joined, they are put together.

lightning A kind of natural electricity that we see as a flash of light in the sky.

motors Machines that make things move.

natural Natural things have not been made by hand or in a factory.

power plants Places where electricity is made.

power The force that makes things move and work.

rail Trains move along metal rails. Rails are also called railway tracks.

robots Machines that can move, light up, make noises, and get work done.

save When you save something, you do not waste it. You only use as much as you need.

shock A sudden blow. A strong electric shock can kill a person.

static If something is static, it does not move. Static electricity stays in one place.

switches Switches turn things on and off.

turbines Machines with blades that spin fast to make electricity.

waste When we waste something, we use more than we need.

wire A long, thin piece of metal. Electricity flows along electric wires.

Index